APR 16 2018

FOX RIVER VALLEY PLD

3 1783 00541 3731

P9-CAY-884

Fox River Valley Libraries
555 Barrington Ave , Dundee, IL 60118
www frvpld info
Renew online or call 847-428-3661

Fact Finders®

CAUSE AND EFFECT: The Bill of Rights

The Second Amendment:
The Right to Bear Arms

BY KIRSTEN W. LARSON

Consultant:
Richard Bell, PhD
Associate Professor of History
University of Maryland, College Park

Fox River Valley PLD
555 Barrington Ave. East Dundee, IL
60118
www.frvpld.info
Renew online or call 847 590-8706

CAPSTONE PRESS
a capstone imprint

Fact Finders Books are published by Capstone Press,
1710 Roe Crest Drive, North Mankato, Minnesota 56003
www.mycapstone.com

Copyright © 2018 by Capstone Press, a Capstone imprint. All rights reserved. No part of this publication may be reproduced in whole or in part, or stored in a retrieval system, or transmitted in any form or by any means, electronic, mechanical, photocopying, recording, or otherwise, without written permission of the publisher.

Library of Congress Cataloging-in-Publication Data
Names: Larson, Kirsten W., author.
Title: The Second Amendment : the right to bear arms / by Kirsten W. Larson.
Description: North Mankato, Minnesota : Capstone Press, 2018. | Series: Fact
    finders. Cause and effect : the Bill of Rights. | Includes bibliographical
    references and index.
Identifiers: LCCN 2017006675
ISBN 978-1-5157-7165-4 (library binding)
ISBN 978-1-5157-7178-4 (paperback)
ISBN 978-1-5157-7183-8 (eBook PDF)
Subjects: LCSH: Firearms—Law and legislation—United States—Juvenile
    literature. | United States. Constitution. 2nd Amendment—Juvenile
    literature.
Classification: LCC KF3941 .L38 2018 | DDC 344.7305/33—dc23
LC record available at https://lccn.loc.gov/2017006675

Editorial Credits
Brenda Haugen, editor; Brent Slingsby, designer; Tracey Engel, media researcher;
Katy LaVigne, production specialist

Source Notes
Page 8, callout: Samuel Adams. *The Writings of Samuel Adams.* Ed. Harry Alonzo Cushing. Vol. 3. New York: G.P. Putnam's Sons, 1907, p. 213.
Page 11, callout: "Pennsylvania Constitution of 1776, Declaration of Rights." The Founders' Constitution: Bill of Rights. University of Chicago. 2000. 25 Oct. 2016. http://press-pubs.uchicago.edu/founders/documents/bill_of_rightss5.html
Page 11, callout: "Constitution of Vermont — July 8, 1777." The Avalon Project: Constitution of Vermont — July 8, 1777. Yale University. 2008. 25 Oct. 2016. http://avalon.law.yale.edu/18th_century/vt01.asp
Page 13, sidebar: "The Constitution of the United States: A Transcription." National Archives and Records Administration. 28 Feb 2017. 30 Nov. 2016. https://www.archives.gov/founding-docs/constitution-transcript#toc-section-8-
Page 15, callout: "Congress Creates the Bill of Rights: Go Inside the First Continental Congress." The National Archives: Center for Legislative Archives. p. 49. 26 Oct. 2016. https://www.archives.gov/files/legislative/resources/bill-of-rights/CCBR_IIB.pdf
Page 16, line 5: "Congress Creates the Bill of Rights: Go Inside the First Continental Congress." The National Archives: Center for Legislative Archives. p. 50. 26 Oct 2016. https://www.archives.gov/files/legislative/resources/bill-of-rights/CCBR_IIB.pdf
Page 16, line 10: "Congress Creates the Bill of Rights: Go Inside the First Continental Congress." The National Archives: Center for Legislative Archives. p. 49. 26 Oct. 2016. https://www.archives.gov/files/legislative/resources/bill-of-rights/CCBR_IIB.pdf
Page 20, line 17: Saul Cornell. "What the 'Right to Bear Arms' Really Means." Salon.com. 15 Jan. 2011. 8 Nov. 2016. http://www.salon.com/2011/01/15/saul_cornell_guns/
Page 27, callout: Antonin Scalia. *District of Columbia vs. Heller* Opinion. U.S. Supreme Court. 26 June 2008. Legal Information Institute. Cornell University Law School. 3 Oct. 2016. https://www.law.cornell.edu/supct/html/07-290.ZS.html/07-290.ZO.html

Photo Credits
Alamy: Ian Dagnall, 13, Maurice Savage, 24; AP Photo: Wilfredo Lee, 25; Getty Images: Bettmann, 20, 23; Newscom: KEVIN DIETSCH/UPI, 27; North Wind Picture Archives, 4, 7, 9, 11; Shutterstock: Everett Historical, 14, 19, 21, Nestudio, cover, Tischenko Irina, cover and interior design element
Design Elements: Shutterstock

Printed and bound in the USA.
010399F17

Table of
Contents

Guns in EARLY AMERICA

Guns have been part of life in America since Europeans arrived in what became the colonies. Colonists shot birds and deer for meat. They had guns to fight American Indians and as part of the **militia**.

The militia was both a police force and an army. Most white men had to serve in the militia when needed. The rest of the time, they farmed or worked at other jobs. Laws kept American Indians and slaves from owning guns.

The militia fought the French and American Indians for control of western lands such as the Ohio Valley. These clashes were known as the French and Indian War (1754–1763). Later, **patriot** militias fought the British during the American Revolution (1775–1783). Ordinary people protected their towns, property, and families through the militia.

Colonists used guns to protect themselves from American Indian attacks.

Many early Americans thought the militia was important for a free country. They feared the power of **professional** armies. They favored part-time troops. These views shaped how the military was dealt with in the Constitution. Still, many wanted to protect the militia further. The Second **Amendment** of the Bill of Rights does that. It also secures the right to own and carry a weapon.

Gun Ownership in the Colonies

Many men and some women in the colonies owned guns. English, French, and Dutch colonies in North America required all white men ages 16 to 60 to join the militia. The men bought their own guns. If men were too poor to do so, they could borrow money from the government to buy weapons.

militia—a group of citizens who are trained to fight, but who only serve in an emergency; today, the National Guard serves as the militia for the United States
patriot—a person who sided with the colonies during the Revolutionary War
professional—a person who makes money doing an activity
amendment—a change made to a law or a legal document

WHY WAS THE
Second Amendment Written?

The Second Amendment grew out of many Americans' fear of harsh rulers. They worried about a **tyrant** using the army to enforce unfair laws. They believed a militia could protect them. To have a militia, people needed arms.

Cause #1: The Use of British Soldiers in the Colonies

From 1754 to 1763, Great Britain fought with France over land in the colonies. The war was costly. King George III of Britain ordered the colonies to help pay the cost. He **taxed** goods such as sugar and tea. Colonists complained.

King George III used British troops to carry out his orders. Extra British troops arrived in Boston in 1768. The colonists pestered the troops. When a worker insulted a soldier in 1770, a fight broke out. During the next few days, more people joined in. British troops eventually fired on an angry crowd. Five people died. Six more were hurt. The event became known as the Boston Massacre.

Still, colonists continued to protest the taxes. They destroyed tea during the Boston Tea Party. To punish them, members of Parliament in Great Britain passed new laws, including the Quartering Act of 1774. The Quartering Act said the people of Boston had to house soldiers in their homes.

tyrant—someone who rules other people in a cruel or unjust way
tax—money collected from a country's citizens to help pay for running the government

The Boston Tea Party

About 60 colonists dressed up as American Indians on December 16, 1773. They sneaked aboard British East India Company ships in Boston Harbor. They destroyed 342 chests of tea that night. Much of it was thrown overboard. In response, the British passed new laws, including the Quartering Act of 1774. Another law closed Boston Harbor to trade. It would reopen when people paid for the ruined tea. Another act gave the king's representative, the colonial governor, more power. These acts further angered the colonists.

FAST FACT:

British troops were called Redcoats because of the red jackets they wore.

Colonists threw tea overboard to protest Great Britain's tax on tea.

Cause #2: The British Army Takes Weapons and Ammunition

As tensions grew, the British tried to keep weapons away from the colonists. King George III forbade sending guns and **ammunition** to America in 1774. The next year, he ordered British troops to take colonists' weapons. Soldiers searched people's homes. They took any arms they found.

The British also raided public buildings where arms and ammunition were stored. They seized gunpowder from a building in Charlestown, Massachusetts, in September 1774.

"They have told us we shall have no more guns, no more powder to use."
—Samuel Adams, 1775, leader of the Boston Tea Party

FAST FACT:

British and colonial troops used the Brown Bess musket during the American Revolution. It was inaccurate and hard to load. Trained men could fire four lead balls per minute.

ammunition—bullets and other objects that can be fired from weapons

Troops tried to take arms stored near Concord, Massachusetts. These included cannons, ammunition, gunpowder, and other supplies. On April 18, 1775, 800 Redcoats marched on Concord from Boston. Paul Revere and others rode on horseback to warn patriots that the troops were coming. The local patriot militia cut off the British at the town of Lexington, Massachusetts. The first shots of the American Revolution were fired. The Redcoats later marched to Concord. They looked for the weapons, but they had been moved. The two sides clashed again, but the British retreated.

A few days later, the British took ammunition in Williamsburg, Virginia. They seized 15 barrels of gunpowder.

Colonial militia members called Minutemen fought in the Battle of Concord.

Cause #3: Earlier Rights to Bear Arms

English colonists enjoyed the right to bear arms well before the United States became a nation. The government in England had passed the English Bill of Rights in 1689. It protected many of the freedoms Americans would later spell out in the U.S. Bill of Rights. The English Bill of Rights protected the right to free speech and **debate**. It also protected the right to bear arms. English colonists had the same rights as people living in England.

When the colonies became the United States, each state wrote its own constitution. Many of the constitutions listed rights people should have. These rights often included freedom of religion. This meant people could worship as they chose. States also protected the freedom of the press. This meant people could not be punished for criticizing the government in newspapers or other writings. Several states protected the right to bear arms. They included Pennsylvania, Vermont, Virginia, North Carolina, and Massachusetts.

debate—a discussion in which people offer different opinions

> "The people have a right to bear arms for the defen[s]e of themselves and the state."
>
> —Pennsylvania Constitution 1776, Declaration of Rights (The Vermont Constitution, A Declaration of the Rights of the Inhabitants of the State of Vermont, 1777, uses the same wording.)

In the 1700s people sometimes read newspapers in library reading rooms.

Cause #4: The Anti-Federalists

Men from 12 of the states came together in 1787 to form a new **federal** government. The U.S. Constitution laid out how the government would work. When the document was finished, the states had to approve it. Anti-Federalists argued against the Constitution. They felt it gave the new government too many powers.

One of these powers was control over the military. The Constitution created both an army and navy. This worried the Anti-Federalists. They remembered how King George III had treated them. He had used the Redcoats to enforce harsh laws.

The Constitution also gave Congress control over the militia. During the American Revolution, military leaders saw that the militia was not well trained. The Founding Fathers hoped giving Congress responsibility for the militia would make the militia stronger. They hoped a strong militia would mean a smaller army.

Still, the Anti-Federalists feared Congress might use its new powers to ruin the militia. They would not approve the Constitution without some protection.

federal—the central government of the United States

The Military and the Constitution

Article I, Section 8, of the Constitution gave Congress the power:

"To raise and support Armies, but no Appropriation of Money to that Use shall be for a longer Term than two Years;

To provide and maintain a Navy;

To make Rules for the Government and Regulation of the land and naval Forces;

To provide for calling forth the Militia to execute the Laws of the Union, suppress Insurrections and repel Invasions;

To provide for organizing, arming, and disciplining, the Militia, and for governing such Part of them as may be employed in the Service of the United States, reserving to the States respectively, the Appointment of the Officers, and the Authority of training the Militia according to the discipline prescribed by Congress."

George Washington (standing right) at the Constitutional Convention

Writing the
SECOND AMENDMENT

George Mason of Virginia first called for a federal bill of rights during the Constitutional Convention in Philadelphia in 1787. Many states had their own bills of rights. A judge, landowner, and politician, Mason had written Virginia's Bill of Rights. But not all delegates to the Constitutional Convention agreed that a federal bill of rights was needed. They argued that most state constitutions included some form of guaranteed rights. Others feared that listing certain rights would suggest that those were the only rights granted to the people. Mason's idea was rejected with little debate.

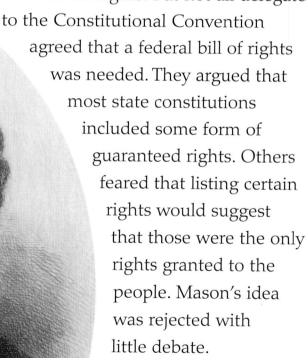

George Mason

The issue arose again when the delegates returned to their states to **ratify** the Constitution. The first five states approved the document easily. Then debates grew more heated. Anti-Federalists argued the Constitution should include a bill of rights. Massachusetts would only approve the Constitution if the new Congress would consider a list of amendments, which included a bill of rights.

Six states — New Hampshire, New York, Virginia, Rhode Island, Massachusetts, and Pennsylvania — specifically called for a right to bear arms in the bill of rights.

The Constitution's author, James Madison of Virginia, wanted to make sure the document was ratified. He agreed to draft a bill of rights. Among the amendments he offered June 8, 1789, was the right to bear arms.

ratify—to approve

"The right of the people to keep and bear arms shall not be infringed; a well armed and well regulated militia being the best security of a free country; but no person religiously scrupulous of bearing arms shall be compelled to render military service in person."

—James Madison's original wording of the Second Amendment, June 8, 1789

The U.S. House of Representatives discussed the Bill of Rights through the summer of 1789. The House put Madison's words in the Second Amendment in a different order. Documents from the time do not say why. The House also changed Madison's words describing the militia. It said the militia was "composed of the body of the people." The House also called it "the best security of a free state." The House approved the Bill of Rights on August 24, 1789. It was now the Senate's turn.

The Senate struck Madison's last words in what became the Second Amendment. He had written, "but no person religiously scrupulous of bearing arms shall be compelled to render military service in person." This protected people whose religious beliefs kept them from fighting, such as **Quakers**. Madison wanted to make sure Quakers did not have to serve in the military. Some senators feared the government would use those words to keep non-Quakers from bearing arms.

After the House agreed with the Senate's changes, Congress approved the Bill of Rights on September 25, 1789. Like the Constitution, the Bill of Rights had to be approved by the state legislatures. This took two years. The Bill of Rights became law in 1791.

Quaker—a member of the Religious Society of Friends — a group founded in the 1600s — who attends silent religious services without a preacher and opposes war

The Bill of Rights

Amendment I

Congress shall make no law respecting an establishment of religion, or prohibiting the free exercise thereof; or abridging the freedom of speech, or of the press; or the right of the people peaceably to assemble, and to petition the government for a redress of grievances.

Amendment II

A well regulated militia, being necessary to the security of a free state, the right of the people to keep and bear arms, shall not be infringed.

Amendment III

No soldier shall, in time of peace be quartered in any house, without the consent of the owner, nor in time of war, but in a manner to be prescribed by law.

Amendment IV

The right of the people to be secure in their persons, houses, papers, and effects, against unreasonable searches and seizures, shall not be violated, and no warrants shall issue, but upon probable cause, supported by oath or affirmation, and particularly describing the place to be searched, and the persons or things to be seized.

Amendment V

No person shall be held to answer for a capital, or otherwise infamous crime, unless on a presentment or indictment of a grand jury, except in cases arising in the land or naval forces, or in the militia, when in actual service in time of war or public danger; nor shall any person be subject for the same offense to be twice put in jeopardy of life or limb; nor shall be compelled in any criminal case to be a witness against himself, nor be deprived of life, liberty, or property, without due process of law; nor shall private property be taken for public use, without just compensation.

Amendment VI

In all criminal prosecutions, the accused shall enjoy the right to a speedy and public trial, by an impartial jury of the state and district wherein the crime shall have been committed, which district shall have been previously ascertained by law, and to be informed of the nature and cause of the accusation; to be confronted with the witnesses against him; to have compulsory process for obtaining witnesses in his favor, and to have the assistance of counsel for his defense.

Amendment VII

In suits at common law, where the value in controversy shall exceed twenty dollars, the right of trial by jury shall be preserved, and no fact tried by a jury, shall be otherwise reexamined in any court of the United States, than according to the rules of the common law.

Amendment VIII

Excessive bail shall not be required, nor excessive fines imposed, nor cruel and unusual punishments inflicted.

Amendment IX

The enumeration in the Constitution, of certain rights, shall not be construed to deny or disparage others retained by the people.

Amendment X

The powers not delegated to the United States by the Constitution, nor prohibited by it to the states, are reserved to the states respectively, or to the people.

What Effects Did the
SECOND AMENDMENT HAVE?

Through the years, the meaning of the right to bear arms has changed. Today it includes the right to own weapons for self-defense.

Effect #1: More People Bear Arms

The Second Amendment spread the right to bear arms to more people. All free white men had the right. In England laws limited **Catholics'** rights to bear arms. They were considered enemies of the **Protestant** kings. Some Catholics settled in the colony of Maryland. A 1744 law there said Catholics could not serve in the militia or have public weapons. The Second Amendment did not limit the right to bear arms based on a person's faith.

Effect #2: Strengthening the Militia

The Second Amendment led to laws to improve the militia. The Uniform Militia Act (1792) said most white men ages 18 to 45 had to serve in the militia. It detailed what arms and ammunition they had to buy. The Calling Forth Act (1792) gave the U.S. president the power to call up the militia. President George Washington called on the state militias in 1794 to put down the Whiskey Rebellion. Pennsylvania farmers were protesting taxes on whiskey. When they set fire to a tax collector's home, Washington assembled 13,000 troops. Fearing a fight, the rebels returned home.

Rebels tar and feather a tax collector and burn his home during the Whiskey Rebellion.

Catholic—a member of the Roman Catholic Church
Protestant—a Christian who does not belong to the Roman Catholic Church or the Orthodox Church

Effect #3: Gun-Control Laws

The Second Amendment led to more state and local gun laws. Many states already kept track of who owned guns. They had rules about where gunpowder could be stored. Still others limited when and where people could carry guns. In Ohio, for example, people could not fire a gun inside the borders of a town. Many states added laws in the 1800s that made it illegal to carry hidden weapons. This included both guns and knives. Massachusetts law said people who rebelled against the state could lose their guns. States such as Massachusetts also outlawed keeping loaded guns at home.

Even the Wild West had gun laws. People could carry guns freely in the country. Yet many frontier towns outlawed guns. In 1873 visitors to Wichita, Kansas, had to leave their guns at the police station. They got their guns back when they left town. Dodge City, Kansas, posted a sign saying, "The Carrying Of Firearms Strictly Prohibited."

Dodge City, Kansas, was a wild frontier town in the days of the Wild West.

Women and Guns

The Second Amendment did not apply to everyone. Laws didn't allow slaves to own guns. Slave owners feared they would use guns to rise up. Historians debate whether the law protected women's rights to bear arms. By law, women could not serve in the militia. Yet many women used guns, especially on the frontier. Women such as Annie Oakley and Martha "Calamity Jane" Canary (right) were expert shooters. Calamity Jane fought American Indians. She also served as an Army scout. Oakley showed off her skills as a sharpshooter in the Wild West Show.

Effect #4: Birth of the National Guard

State militias served in wars through the 1800s. Often the troops did not receive enough money for training and equipment. Yet protecting the militia remained an important American idea. A set of laws in the early 1900s improved the militia. They gave states federal money for weapons and training. They made sure all troops used the same equipment. By 1916 the militia, now called the National Guard, became part of the U.S. Army.

FAST FACT:

During the American Revolution, Frenchman Marquis de Lafayette helped defeat the British at the Battle of Yorktown. Lafayette first used the term "national guard" in 1824. The U.S. militia took the name National Guard in 1916.

Effect #5: National Firearms Act of 1934

The 1934 National Firearms Act was the first federal law to limit guns. Gun violence had increased in the 1930s. Men such as Al Capone and John Dillinger fought rival gangs. The 1934 law controlled some guns, such as machine guns and sawed-off shotguns that were used by gangs. Many wondered if the law violated the Second Amendment. In 1939 the Supreme Court ruled on the issue. It said the Second Amendment does not protect a person's right to own guns for personal defense. The Firearms Act could stand. This view continued for about 70 years.

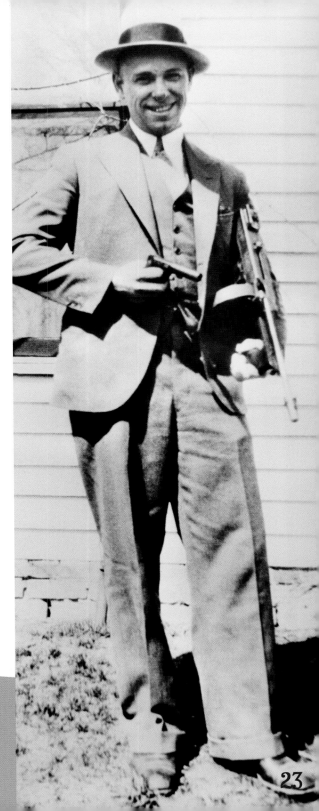

John Dillinger posed with a Colt .38 in one hand and a submachine gun in the other shortly before he was killed.

Effect #6: The NRA Protects the Second Amendment

During the Civil War (1861–1865), military officers were upset by their troops' poor shooting skills. Some Civil War **veterans** formed the National Rifle Association in 1871. Their goal was to promote shooting practice. The NRA set up gun ranges. There, people could practice shooting targets. The NRA also held shooting contests. These continue today.

As the country changed, so did the NRA. Increased gun violence in the 1960s led to more gun laws. When Lee Harvey Oswald **assassinated** President John F. Kennedy on November 22, 1963, people were angry because Oswald had bought his gun through the mail.

As Congress worked to pass new gun laws, the NRA fought back. It protested new laws. The group called for all members to write to their lawmakers. When the Gun Control Act of 1968 finally passed, it did so after being considerably weakened by the NRA. The group helped stop rules requiring that people get gun licenses. The NRA also helped strike rules requiring people to register their guns. Soon after the gun law passed, the NRA's goal became the total defense of the Second Amendment.

The Brady Bill

The 1994 Brady Bill boosted federal gun laws. It was named for James Brady, who pushed for the law. He was the White House press secretary under President Ronald Reagan. When gunman John Hinckley tried to assassinate Reagan in 1981, Brady was hurt along with the president. Both Brady and Reagan survived, but Brady spent the rest of his life partially paralyzed, requiring the full-time use of a wheelchair.

The Brady Bill created a five-day waiting period for people buying guns at most stores. This gave police time to do background checks. The goal was to keep dangerous people from buying weapons.

Some members of Congress tried to expand background checks through a new law in 2013. It would have required background checks for guns bought at gun shows or on the Internet. It failed.

President Bill Clinton (right) met with James Brady on the first anniversary of the Brady handgun conrol law.

veteran—a person who served in the armed forces
assassinate—murder, often for political reasons

Effect #7: *District of Columbia v. Heller* (2008)

The Supreme Court changed its view of the Second Amendment in 2008. Before 2008 the court had said that people only had a right to arms as part of the militia. Now the court said that guns used for personal defense were protected too.

Security guard Dick Heller was at the center of the 2008 Supreme Court case. He had a gun at work at the Federal Judicial Center. He wanted to keep a handgun at his Washington, D.C., home for safety. Laws in that city kept people from owning handguns. They could own long guns, such as rifles, but they had to be taken apart or locked and stored.

The Supreme Court said the city's laws took away Heller's right to bear arms. The Court struck down the D.C. law. Still, the Court said, some gun bans were okay. For example, machine guns could be banned. Laws keeping criminals from owning guns were okay too, according to the Court's ruling.

"There seems to us no doubt, on the basis of both text and history, that the Second Amendment conferred an individual right to keep and bear arms."

—Chief Justice Antonin Scalia, *D.C. v. Heller*, opinion of the Supreme Court, 2008

Dick Heller spoke outside the Supreme Court Building after the Court heard arguments in his case.

The Second Amendment
TODAY

Many people still argue about the Second Amendment. New gun laws spark much debate. Recent polls show half of Americans think gun-control laws are important. At the same time, slightly less than half say the right to bear arms must be guarded.

Overall, gun violence in the United States has dropped since the 1990s. Yet in the last 10 years, the number of **mass shootings** has gone up. A lone shooter killed 49 people in 2016 at a nightclub in Orlando, Florida. It was the most deadly shooting in U.S. history.

Each mass shooting leads to calls for new gun laws. After the Orlando shooting, people called for a ban on **assault weapons**. Such guns were outlawed from 1994 to 2004.

The number of gun owners in the United States has dropped. Only about a third of homes have at least one gun. Still, Americans own far more guns than people in any other nation. By 2016 the number of guns in the United States totaled more than 300 million. That's about twice as many guns per person as there were in 1968. And that's nearly equal to the U.S. population, which is about 318.9 million.

mass shooting—an event in which four or more people are killed or hurt by guns
assault weapon—a type of semi-automatic gun designed to kill quickly and efficiently

Americans and Gun Laws

A June 2016 CNN poll asked Americans which gun laws they support.

* About 92 percent said people buying a gun should be checked for prior crimes.
* 87 percent said criminals or people with mental illness should not be able to own guns.
* 54 percent said they do not want people owning machine-gun-type weapons.

Gun Ownership Around the World (2007)

RANK	COUNTRY	NUMBER OF GUNS PER 100 PEOPLE
1	United States	88.8
2	Yemen	54.8
3	Switzerland	45.7
4	Finland	45.3
5	Serbia	37.8
13	Canada	30.8

GLOSSARY

amendment (uh-MEND-muhnt)—a change made to a law or a legal document

ammunition (am-yoo-NI-shuhn)—bullets and other objects that can be fired from weapons

assassinate (uh-SASS-uh-nate)—murder, often for political reasons

assault weapon (uh-SAWLT WEP-un)—a type of semi-automatic gun designed to kill quickly and efficiently

Catholic (KATH-uh-lik)—a member of the Roman Catholic Church

debate (di-BAYT)—a discussion in which people offer different opinions

federal (FED-ur-uhl)—the central government of the United States

mass shooting (MASS SHOO-ting)—an event in which four or more people are killed or hurt by guns

militia (muh-LISH-uh)—a group of citizens who are trained to fight, but who only serve in an emergency; today, the National Guard serves as the militia for the United States

patriot (PAY-tree-uht)—a person who sided with the colonies during the Revolutionary War

professional (pruh-FESH-uh-nuhl)—a person who makes money doing an activity

Protestant (PROT-uh-stuhnt)—a Christian who does not belong to the Roman Catholic Church or the Orthodox Church

Quaker (KWAY-kur)—a member of the Religious Society of Friends — a group founded in the 1600s — who attends silent religious services without a preacher, and opposes war

ratify (RAH-tuh-fye)—to approve

tax (TAKS)—money collected from a country's citizens to help pay for running the government

tyrant (TYE-ruhnt)—someone who rules other people in a cruel or unjust way

veteran (VET-ur-uhn)—a person who served in the armed forces

READ MORE

Baxter, Roberta. *The Bill of Rights.* Documenting U.S. History. Chicago: Heinemann Library, 2013.

Krull, Kathleen. *A Kids' Guide to America's Bill of Rights.* New York: Harper, 2015.

Leavitt, Amie Jane. *The Bill of Rights in Translation: What It Really Means.* Kids' Translations. Mankato, Minn.: Capstone Press, 2017.

INTERNET SITES

Use FactHound to find Internet sites related to this book.

Visit *www.facthound.com*

Just type in 9781515771654 and go.

 Check out projects, games and lots more at
www.capstonekids.com

CRITICAL THINKING QUESTIONS

1. Why do you think the Second Amendment was changed to protect guns used for personal defense?

2. Using the photos and sidebars along with the text, discuss how gun control has changed since colonial times.

3. What if the militia had been more effective during the Revolutionary War? How would that have affected the need for the Second Amendment?

INDEX